JAN 1 4 1993

D0437583

BOOKS BY MONA VAN DUYN

Firefall

FIREFALL

POEMS

Mona Van Duyn

Public Library San Mateo, CA

ALFRED A. KNOPF

New York

1993

THIS IS A BORZOI BOOK
PUBLISHED BY ALFRED A. KNOPF, INC.

Copyright © 1992 by Mona Van Duyn

All rights reserved under International and Pan-American Copyright Conventions. Published in the United States by Alfred A. Knopf, Inc., New York, and simultaneously in Canada by Random House of Canada Limited, Toronto. Distributed by Random House, Inc., New York.

POEMS IN THESE PAGES HAVE APPEARED IN:

The Cream City Review: "Fallen Angel"
First Line: "For Julia Li Qiu"
The Formalist: "Christmas Present for a Poet," "Commencement," "Late Flight of the Love God," "The Poet Reconciles Herself to Politicians," "Eruption"
Iowa Woman: "Caps," "Late Wishes"
The Nation: "Emergency Room (Turnpike, Anywhere, USA)"
The New Republic: "Chagall's 'Les Plumes en Fleur' ", "At the Mall"
The New Virginia Review: "Struggle Toward a Narrative"
The New Yorker: "The Marriage Sculptor," "A Dog Lover's Confession," "The Delivery," "Rascasse"
The New York Times: "Summer Virus"
The North American Review: "From the Mantel," "Have You Seen Me?," "One Strategy for Loving the World"
Parnassus: "Poets' Paint Pots"
Poetry: "For May Swenson," "Insiders," "Closures," "The Beginning," "Long Stretch," "A Passing Thought," "Mr. and Mrs. Jack Sprat in the Kitchen," "Extra Time"
Poetry Northwest: "Miranda Grows Up," "A Certain Age"
The Southern Review: "Addendum to 'The Block' ", (under the title "Our Block")
The University of the South Theological Journal: "Je Meurs de Soif Auprès de la Fontaine," "Another Tempest"
The Yale Review: "Words for the Dumb," "Endings"
The Breadloaf Anthology of Nature Poetry (Univ. Press of New England): "Poets in Late Winter"

Library of Congress Cataloging-in-Publication Data

Van Duyn, Mona.
    Firefall : poems / Mona Van Duyn.—1st ed.
      p. cm.
    ISBN 0-679-41897-0
    I. Title.
PS3543.A563F57   1993
811'.54—dc20

92-17163
CIP

Manufactured in the United States of America
First Edition

For JARVIS *and* HARRY

The perilous Pass was blocked
by the blackness in which we die,
but their strong and steady hearts
shone out and passed by.

CONTENTS

Contents

I

On Olympus Art's mother
keeps her pet, place and show
hard to judge as a star,
but here, loving each other,
it's easy to know
who the real winners are.

> *from* LONG STRETCH

A DOG LOVER'S CONFESSION*

Perfect love I have known,
whose animal eyes
disregard all disguise,
go beyond flesh and bone,

an unshaken forever,
heart's white purity
any angel would envy.
But I slightly prefer

unpredictable pairing,
pain and peace in one thing,
unplumbable thoughts,
the love that comes wearing,
fall, fire, freeze or spring,
black and white polka dots.

* See note 1 on page 83

CHAGALL'S "LES PLUMES EN FLEUR"

At first glimpse an unearthly efflorescence,
exquisite spray, drift, swirl. The lightest
touch or heaviness of breath would blow
delicate blushes of blue pink lemon snow

apart from the high white stamen-head that offers
some essence of the flowering self to another.
Or, at second glance, a fair head rising
from a nest of the very self, comb-capped, surprising,

the head of a hen, beak open, uttering
with perfect openness its messages,
the river of blood that rises from heart to word
dyeing with carmine the chaste neck of the bird.

The eye in the profiled head is huge and black.
Above and beyond lie the many valences
of darkness; that dark has poured into the well-pit
of eye, whose deep holding has gentled it.

Receiving the gift to his eyes and ears, a horse
leans in from the dark, his head half-bowed, too shy
to show the fiery surge of his love and pleasure.
Half-dreading to look, abashed, he has turned to azure.

For who can take in the full splendor of self
when it opens the door and, feathery as a light,
reveals itself to the waiting, uncandled one,
its voice arising out of its heavenly home-spun?

And how can my heavy pen bring forth a shimmering
word for this beauty of self displayed in friendship?
Then *Prêtez-moi*, I pray, *pour écrire un mot*,
la plume, birds-in-blossom, *mes Pierrots!*

MR. AND MRS. JACK SPRAT IN THE KITCHEN

"About half a box,"
I say, and the male
weighs his pasta sticks
on our postal scale.

To support my sauce
of a guesswork rhymer
he boils by the laws
of electric timer.

Our joint creation,
my searchings, revisions,
tossed with his ration
of compulsive precisions,

so mimics life
we believe it mandated
that God had a wife
who collaborated.

And cracked, scraped, old,
still the bowl glows gold.

"JE MEURS DE SOIF AUPRÈS DE LA FONTAINE"

an hommage *for John Hollander*

Duke, there are deserts with fountains where lovers tarry
and those who die of thirst at the fountain-side,
since for love to be real it must first be imaginary.

Out of deathly dryness rises its adversary,
the perfect idea whose passion will never subside—
in the desert, Duke, a fountain where lovers tarry.

No groom can grasp those diamonds, leaping and airy,
and each faceted drop would cut the throat of a bride,
though for love to be real it must first be imaginary.

The immortal poem of love may merely miscarry,
the saddled camels kneel and wait, untried
in those deserts, Duke, with fountains where lovers tarry,

trapped in a dream of art which, weeping or merry
fills up the heart and cannot be denied,
since for love to be real it must first be imaginary.

Yes, for love to be real it must first be imaginary,
but Duke, there are deserts with fountains where lovers tarry,
dying of thirst, who never will mount and ride
to the green oasis where word and water marry.

---

* In the 15th century the Duc d'Orleans set a villanelle contest for poets, all of whom were to use the line "I die of thirst here at the fountain-side"—an inspired line which still reverberates in the imagination of present-day poets.

MIRANDA GROWS UP

Prospero
foreknew
what snow
could do:
half-kill
the beguiled,
heart-chill
his child.

But she
forgave
what swirled

on every
brave
new world.

ONE STRATEGY FOR LOVING THE WORLD

To accept this vale
I have had to believe
every death must entail
leaving someone to grieve.

Starved beggar, DeathRow man,
street drunk or O.D.,
beaten child or bought woman,
unclaimed refugee,

though no stone rolls away
let one cross that they bore be:
a life that's now clay
never read its own story.

Deep lies the fossil
manuscript, still unbleached,
of its truest witness,

some loving apostle
whose gospel never reached
that heart's printing press.

FOR JULIA LI QIU

(and Lijun and Cho)

Ten days before we expected you, we gave
your mother and father fish and shrimp chowder
(in carp bowls, with Cloud Ears swimming in it darkly
—a bow to your heritage) lemon pie and tea.

Next morning, early, the telephone: "Surprise!
We're in the labor room. Water broke.
I think baby want chowder, want to come quickly,
but may take twenty-four hours. Talk now to Lili."

"Not so good now. Pain." Your mother had learned
English in classes here by leaps and bounds.
(Your poet father, translator of Eliot and Pound,
had come first, plunging his lines in the foreign sound.)

Tall, slim, lovely, young, she let us
lead her to cut-rate dress sales, to necklaces
and earrings she'd never had. ("Dressed up, she ask me
(so young!) 'Why you not write of love, of Lili?' ")

Her pregnancy, so far from home, found her mother
unable to get a visa, no one to help
but your father. Putting classes and Yaddo "on hold,"
he gave himself to the strange steeps of a threshold.

Through the endless night and day our "daughter" labored
in the alien, inconceivable, cruel land
her body had turned to, believing that finally
she could bring you with her into love's gentler country.

Your mother and father alone. No genes gave us leave
to be near. But friendship's telephone let me hear,
when nothing the childbirth classes taught them came true,
your father calling over and over to you:

9

For Julia Li Qiu

"Come to the garden of life, its stony walkways
through rampant blossoms of glory and peace, its dappled
light and shade for the spirit's exquisite wooing.
There is nothing for you in death's dark fields of undoing.

"Come, come to love's tragi-comedy,
the masterpiece re-written for every body
and soul, its tears and laughter as near to each other
as Hell and Heaven are, as lover and brother.

"Come to my heart, my poems. Come to this world.
Take the gigantic bouquet the trees are bringing,
a flaring palette of joy, take the great spendthrift
spangle of diamond necklaces, your gift

from the sky. Come, my dearest stranger, my daughter,
find with me and your mother the metaphors
that make us meld, come to the needy hearts
and chill future that want your flame, to the living arts."

You came, slowly, clear to the open door.
For two hours your father saw your black hair.
"Can't come out. They say that perhaps baby
too big. Now they must operate on my Lili."

"Don't worry." "Don't *you* worry" So brave our girl,
in terror, pain, strangeness, exhaustion, she gives
still more of self. "The child will be beautiful, Cho,
from the first moment. It's best for Lili, they know."

"Lots of black hair! She really look like a girl!
But so many tubes in Lili!" While your mother lay
vomiting from anesthetic and weakness,
we found garage-sale things, and through the excess

of American stores I followed young mothers for clothing.
In champagne and tea we toasted you and cooed
with your father through nursery glass at you in your manger.
("Are you the grandmother?" "I wish I were!") "Now no danger,

but, so funny, I can't believe it's true. Is it real
(*Lili* believe, keep wanting baby, though doctors
say don't hold too long yet) from broken water
I hold in my arms a beautiful black-haired daughter?"

ADDENDUM TO "THE BLOCK"*

"Three new babies are due all at once on the block,"
our soft-hearted widow tells us, walking her fat,
puffing poodle with a new pink bow on her ear.
"Two on the other side of the street, one here."

Within a week three front-step railings blossom
with pink or blue balloons and bold-faced signs
(commercial aids to displaying the shy new joy)
announcing that IT'S A GIRL or IT'S A BOY.

When one celebration comes down, it reveals a mourner.
A small, black dog runs up "to *everyone*,
all day," says the neighbor, and pleads for babying.
"Her nose is out of joint, poor little thing."

Soon, up and down both sidewalks, three black nannies
(two fat, one thin), each pushing a pristine carriage,
acquaint themselves with each other, paint high-pitched rainbows
of giggles and gossip over the street's doze.

The few old-timers, out for their therapeutic
heart-walks, glare or coo into a carriage
as suits their hearts: "More noise, clutter, *coping*,"
or "More life to wrap one's self in, breath, *hoping*."

Before we know it, dangling by his wrist
from the hand of a leaning mother, one infant lurches
as far as our drive, legs testing this strange notion,
toes touching or missing the ground, eyes wild with promotion.

Much later a crowd chooses our street to parade
"ABORTION KILLS BABIES," their frozen faces
grim, their kids in strollers grim, as if we,
the human block, were beneath reality.

* The poem "The Block" appears in my preceding book, *Near Changes.*

Raked leaves in heaps lie at the curb for pickup.
Soon the cold will keep secret behind each door
pain, pleasure, vital or lifeless conceptions,
boundless scopes or chilling circumscriptions.

This morning, though, the sun sends a wordless, warm
hug to us all—children, parents, barren
couples, frail graybeards, gays—"hello? good-bye?"
reaching out of the newborn blue of the sky.

THE MARRIAGE SCULPTOR

For Stephen and Mary

As we wandered, bored, in the halls of The Great Museum,
we came upon a late work of the sculptor
which made us stop and catch our breaths, so fine
the embrace of spirits, so expressive the bright pour

of leaning light, so rich the exchanging changes.
"One of his finest!" we all said, and brought
its image as souvenir to dangle before us.
In time, Time's tempests struck what had been wrought.

The piece, we saw, dispirited, was splintered
into wild beams that wildly searched through a dark
where changes lay in scatters. Then we saw
the sculptor, the old master, disembark.

Blind to us all, he turned his rapt face
to the wreck. "Safe. My materials, safe. All.
Now I must start my making. I see it—spirit,
light, change—more brilliant and powerful,

a larger work." Nothing human is perfect,
we thought. What can shelter the next from storm?
He spoke tenderly to his elements: "Beauty
learns from beauty, the first costly form

lies coiled in the last." Then, "I am not Eros.
Since Time is made out of it (who calls himself king)
the human stuff *I* work with is stronger than Time,"
he said to us, who thought we had lost something.

THE BEGINNING

The end
of passion
may refashion
a friend.

Eyes meet
in fear
of such dear
defeat.

The heart's core,
unbroken,
cringes.

The soul's door
swings open
on its hinges.

ERUPTION

How the world justly wakes
under warm-hearted sun—
love remolding mistakes,
slow-ripening passion!

But trapped love can't stop,
will swell to a mountain
till time blows its top
and it scalds everyone.

Its blistering spills,
its molten arrears
leave forms burned apart,
leave hardening chills.

How the world justly fears
the Vesuvius heart!

CHRISTMAS PRESENT FOR A POET

"The shirt you gave me made me look like
a hornet! And the only word I can think
of that rhymes with "hornet" is "hairnet."

That Henley I sent you was certainly never meant
to disguise a loving heart as a hate-filled hornet!
Your friend can only offer her old excuse
for sending a black with yellow stripes—it's hernit-
wit bargain buying. But seeing golden bars
as restraints on dark might strike a sweeter, highernote
of appreciation: golden bars of a form
in poetry, for example, that, like a hairnet,
holds flyaway passion and pain: appearances,
manners, that keep the poor, keep even the whoreneat.
Or hope lighting *any* black. No knitted bargain,
of course, comes near the shirt I might like to hireknit
out of the delicate yarns of dearness and dream.
But the war between world and word goes on, and how'reneut-
rals to find a shop that still is stocked with goods?
And as Life tells dawn every day, it was just not Hernight:
Her people wake up with a belly-ache. Her loners,
as always, drink their near-beer without even a herenut;
everyone wants the moon's green cheese; Her lovers
swallow a camel of fire and strain at a hoargnat.
Why go on? She keeps asking the thin streaks of sunlight.
There are none so deaf as those who deliberately hearnot,
none so blind as those who can't see themselves
as hoer, Knight or middleman, but as horrornaught.
She goes on though, making the best of a bargain world
that offers no chance to change or undo a hueorknot,
braking (with cuss) for the old pedestrian year,
yet finding each New Year something to blow a hornat,
trying to keep the human head-dress of problems
simple in line and solution, no matter howornate,
inept at cleaning each global mess, but removing
Herself with tact from those who can't bear to stay hereinit,
and each time She screws up, trying to separate
those who'renot mad from those who are mad as a hornet.

ANOTHER TEMPEST

Our heart-shaped island, rounded with sea-space
as are our little lives with sleep,
throbbed with storms or magical spells,
lay light or heavy on the deep.

My muse and father, Prospero,
(for the witch or devil parents of nightmare
fairy tales drifted long ago,
useless, outgrown, into thin air)

was the good father a greedy daughter
hopes for, just, loving, kind,
teacher and god in one, now ancient
(we'd all grown old on the isle), half-blind,

but, cloaked, with beard, book and staff
still the powerful source of fertile
murmurings, movements, melodies
of the mind. I ran but could not hurtle

at his bidding, being unwinged,
but he asked little, gave slight direction:
hear and see the airs of this ground,
its caves, glades, springs, with affection.

How had we come together here?
Only Prospero could tell.
Saving us from some worldly wreck,
he tossed me into the floating shell

of a box, added a toddling boy,
pushed with his head to land, life,
raised us from rivalry to love,
and through Ferdinand made me a wife.

And how found we our dear Ariel?
My father smiles and sets great store
by Ariel's own account. Caught
in the cleft of a pine (his metaphor)

he suffered years before my father
came and with his secret art
made the pine gape to let him out.
"My muse!" Ariel cried from the start.

No mirrors reflected our happiness.
We saw what we were in the smile, tear,
frown, surprise of one another.
Act was image, faithful and clear.

My Ferdinand tended the isle,
melted frosts with clever flames,
fired my body with his body,
turned to gardens our rarest claims,

guided stream and sun and shade,
teaching our tender ground to grow,
and, so our withered mage could bloom,
lent his strength to Prospero.

I, love-lotioned, knew my soft,
slow, heavy earthiness.
Life lifted me, though not aloft.
I cradled my blessings, and could bless.

Feet on the ground, ear to the ground,
hearing it, sweet, implacable,
feeling it solid, fragile, sound,
at Prospero's nod my page was full.

All light and aether was Ariel.
Deeply we loved and needed each other.
He was my lost transcendence, grace,
my twin, my other self, my brother.

At our muse's point, arm-wave or wink
his brilliance flashed over land and sea,
releasing each word whose power was trapped
and hidden as *he'd* been in his tree.

The raging seas he could lull to sleep
or with knives of lightning slice the sky.
Revels were begun or ended
in the great spells that he lived by.

As more and more my old father
napped in his cell, Ariel tried
small tricks of his own, a practice show,
for our muse had arranged that when he died

Ariel's life touch eternity,
that his be the sacred book, staff, cloak,
and, enchanter of the great globe itself,
his be the magic all invoke.

One day in the garden as I stood
close to Ferdinand's side, dreaming
his dream of harvest, with a wild shout
Ariel woke us, bright grin gleaming,

leading from the sea a file
of creatures, young, both dark and fair,
wafted, perhaps, from some broken ship,
sea-salt sparkling in their hair,

skin coral from the sun, bodies
tall, trim, bones built to change
the shape, the weight of our home-made island
into something rich and strange.

"I brought them for you!" The "you" hung,
wavering, in the small space between us.
I turned to Ferdinand. His eyes
had widened like an owl's. Nonplus

gave way to tremulous hope, to wonder.
His kiss-closed lips parted. "*Oh brave
new world!*" he called with joy. I felt
chilled breath swirl outward from our love-cave.

I looked in his eyes and saw a snout
break from the water, scaly, gray,
then a whole monstrous otherness
followed, and on his gold pools lay.

My hard paw sank the sun. A scrim
of dusk dimmed down each glowing man.
Toneless, he mouthed our evening hymn:
"It's time for bed, dear Caliban."

MYOPIA

In nearsighted love
if one's not near
with no slightest move
she can disappear.

Their visions are mixed.
Devotion can't steer
if one course be fixed
while the other veer.

She believes what he sees.
Heaven's clearer in sun.
Who could seriously
trust a heart to someone

who knows perfectly well
though not with her eyes
that he glitters above,
and though all the stars fell
out of all of the skies
he would still be her love?

WORDS FOR THE DUMB

*A woman always tries to give her children whatever it
is she feels she missed in life. Sometimes you don't know
what it is till you see what she is trying to give them.
With some it's money, with others it's education, with
others still, it's love.* FRANK O'CONNOR

And if there are no children? The same gear
engages her life for roads up the mountain mirage.
At the breast of her reassurance the small boys'
eyes of a young mate slowly close and dislodge
the hurt some clumsy day jammed in their shining.
With aging, band-aids for the little cuts
and burns of friends become her steady business.
Later she cares, but carefully not too much,
for her friends' children, who run to hug her knees
or lift their arms to be held. But this, after all,
is too much, too much comes pouring toward the only
open vessel—feet too big for the small,
wobbly legs, ears that drag the ground,
undiapered, untrained rear with flailing tail.
A black handful that sleeps on her lap, standing
on hind legs and scratching with needle nails
to get back, growing by coonhound leaps and bounds
to fit his feet, too soon stepping right onto
the lap and curling tight to fit until
his seventy pounds numbs her. But she too
wants the warm weight. Then come full-grown days
he strains to a tighter curl but, relaxing asleep,
falls off one side or the other, trying over
and over until the mystery too deep
for him to fathom makes him lay his chin
each day on her knees, brown eyes, browed with tan
pumpkin seeds, gazing into her own,
puzzled, imploring. She smiles, tears' veteran.

Unidentified quotations are from J. O. Bailey, *The Poetry of Thomas Hardy* (University of North Carolina Press, 1970), and Horace Gregory, *Amy Lowell* (Thomas Nelson, 1958).

Words for the Dumb

A poet read on a poet's face the Hymn:

> SIEGFRIED SASSOON: "When Hardy looked at Wessex his face was suffused with gentle compassion for all living creatures whom he longed to defend against the chanceful injustice and calamity of earthly existence."

For Hardy too the pure, essential fountain
came pouring, pouring, leaping and falling on him
whom others saw as nuisance, terror, good-
for-nothing wire-haired devotee of whim.

> "... so petted by the Hardys and allowed so much freedom that dozens of visitors commented on his behavior." J. M. BARRIE: "a strain to the guests at dinner by walking about *on* the table and taking their food." LADY CYNTHIA ASQUITH: "contesting every forkful of food on its way to my mouth." J. M. BARRIE (who accompanied Hardy and Wessex to a rehearsal of the dramatization of *Tess*): "When it came time when he knew the wireless would be putting on 'The Children's Hour,' his favorite program, Wessex howled so that Hardy had to desert Tess and hurry home with him." MRS. HARDY: "He bit the postman (three times) and he will no longer deliver mail here. . . . Wessex *will* sleep on the sofa and has appropriated a chair for himself in the drawing room."

Within a circle, seated at attention,
(of Jack, John, Tommy, Columbine,
Rosine, Mary and Lydia), poets and critics,
guests of Amy and her canines, dine.

> "After dinner, guests were ushered into deep, comfortable chairs, and each was given a large, clean bathtowel to spread across the knees—protection from pawings and droolings—and caused to feed the sheepdogs their top round of beef. Amy Lowell appeared to be in command of a small kingdom where the distinction between guests and friendly sheepdogs had nearly disappeared."

"When Amy travelled to New Hampshire with her dogs, a local doctor was infuriated to discover he had been called from bed to attend several ailing dogs."

"Maxwell Bodenheim, who came two hours early for dinner, found the dogs on the front lawn. Frightened, he ran, and the playful dogs pursued him and leaped on him, tearing his already ragged coat. Miss Lowell gave him $10. for the damage. Bodenheim demanded $100."

Nature, who in her blessed extravagance,
her inexhaustible presents for heart and eye,
could not be expected to think of every detail
that might afflict them before their time to die,
and so made the mistake that aches through the ages,
scarring young, old, sometimes again
and again—the terrible disparity
in lifelines of love-linked creatures, dogs and men.

"Wessex was buried in the animal graveyard at Max Gate, which already had 12 or 13 dogs and cats, each with his tombstone." Hardy wrote to Sir Sidney Cockerell, "Of course he was only a dog and not a good dog always. But I . . . hope no one will ask me about him or mention his name."

In his late *Winter Words* the still-audible voice of Wessex sounds:

> Should you call as when I knew you,
>   Wistful ones,
>
> . . . .
>
> Should you call as when I knew you,
> I shall not turn to view you,
> I shall not listen to you,
>   Shall not come.

"World War I rationing put an end to the Sevenels order of steak for the seven sheepdogs. Some died, some became so sick they had to be destroyed, from badly preserved horse meat."

Words for the Dumb

De Quincey needed no opium to know
"how blended and intertwisted in this life
are occasions of laughter and tears." And no more likely
occasion than when the lover, with love's knife
stuck in his heart, his face painted simpleton,
sings his ardent aria of farewell
to the loved one the audience knew all along to be
four-legged, under the costume of a belle.

In the pets' cemetery at the Bombay Governor's Palace this tombstone is a favorite of tourists:

LINDY LOO
1932–1943
HER TAIL STILL WAGS
IN OUR HEARTS

And in the human cemetery in Key West, Florida:

SUNNY OTTO
BELOVED YORKSHIRE TERRIER
OF
GENE AND ANNE OTTO
HER BEAUTIFUL LITTLE SPIRIT
WAS A CHALLENGE TO LOVE

It is like, if one were to say what it is like,
what a traveller came upon, a long hot way
beyond a tiny, lonely village, somewhere
Mediterranean. On foot, astray,
seeking a new page for his book of adventures,
he finds what might be trail, turns, winds,
pushes through thorns, head-high leaves, past traces
of other trails, and in a small clearing finds
        something inexplicable. Leaned atilt
        against a rock, a weather-battered statue,
        the Virgin, no doubt, her plaster chapped and cracked,
        faded except for garish streaks of blue

and red, with raddled face that must have been painted
gaudy as a streetwalker. Propped near
is a sign, hand-lettered, with the date and claim
of someone who saw, or thought he saw, a tear
on her cheek for a moment, under the glaring sun.
Before her broken toes a patch remains
of knelt-down weeds, and off to the side of that
a little pile of discarded crutches and canes.

Cathedral love, in the hushed greatness of gold
and lovely tints of rainbow, kneeling down
in illusion's flickering candlelight, may see,
or hope to see, time itself uncrowned,
replaced by the eternal; and the font,
never empty of its holy store,
may bathe the eyes that they may see the world
as no one but the gods have seen it before.
But here, surrounded by derision's brambles
and weeds, a humble image that reveals
of the priceless welling one drop only, somehow
continues to work its own miracle, heals.

"HAVE YOU SEEN ME?"

(Lost Children Ads)

My face in your mail
is no longer me.
Stranger, don't fail
to look carefully,

hear the hopeless, mild
query each day,
"Where is the child
that was taken away?"

Imperceptibly
the world's being taught.

No one can see
what I saw or thought.

Someone wants me
to be where I'm not.

LATE FLIGHT OF THE LOVE GOD

In one late dart,
exhausted, blind,
he missed a heart
and lit in a mind,

a huge, open shelf
full of rustling things.
He lost himself
among other wings.

When he opened his eyes
his wings had grown
for undreamed-of-skies.
He had never known

so rich a rest,
an aim so blest.

SUMMER VIRUS

Send this blaze still higher.
Degree by degree
let my fever aspire
to transfigure me

to a lampbulb's wire,
the red waft of a kite.
From no former fire
shone a blush so bright.

I'll stoke with my numbing
flesh, senses, insight,
unafraid of becoming
more and more light,

since I've felt one presence
as incandescence.

II

At the least touch of any sense, gates to Infinity are ready to fly open. WILLIAM ALLINGHAM

Infinity is fa-ar out! GRAFITTI IN ST. LOUIS

PASSING THOUGHT

She intended to sit there, awake but thinking of noth-
ing in particular . . . until it would be time to start
preparing for bed. But it is hard to think of nothing
in particular after 87 years. Out of all those jumbled
decades heaped up behind, something will worm itself
to the surface. CELIA FREMLIN, *A Lovely Way to Die*

It must be peaceful to come to the end
of the writing, or need for writing, poems,
to wholly let go, like a cat on a lap,
heavy and boneless as unbaked bread dough,
of that constant attentiveness to the sea,
all weathers and tides, its bland seething.
Alert as if no others watched,
as if there had never been another
watcher, driven to know precisely
what is being uncovered or covered
if its near, sluggish graceless barings
show glint, slither, in the old weeds,
or afar, if from under the dark spread
with its tiny wavery quilting, there erupts
something that ducks down under again.
And, if envisioned, the ecstatic strain
and suspense of a try at validation
of mollusc, redworm, mermaid, monster,
something unseen because not looked at
or so brilliantly seen it died into fable,
something nobody knew for sure
was there, and nobody needed to know!
And unending doubt! Could one bring it back
(on the leader of a glimpse so slight,
handling the deep play so unsurely,)
to the world, to its own true tremble of light?

It must be like just before a vacation,
the supper a careless improvising,
a soupkettle crammed with disparate leftovers,
everything kept, even dregs of wine,

bubbling together, the pot unwatched.
Those remnants of past, so much still good,
swell the soup with garbled excitement.
But when the chaos spits something up
which goes over the side and lands on the stove—
the spraddled fern of celery top,
bloodclot of an over-ripe tomato,
tough twig of splurged-on country ham slice—
the pure accident of its splat
is wiped quickly, guiltlessly away,
being nothing more meaningful than that.

COMMENCEMENT

For Howard Nemerov

In the mute beginning
the Word was with God
until human sinning
turned its power to a rod.

But Beauty rose then.
The rod comforts our ways
and earth smiles once again
from the poets' praise.

While he's hooded and gowned
a storm from afar
sends down love of creation
as the heavens resound
for earth's radiant star
with their standing ovation.

LONG STRETCH

For Howard Nemerov

You were out of town
for the smashing surprise:
my head's heavy disguise
in a Pulitzer crown.

The massed flowers that poured in
spread a grave undertaking
on the word-wrestling ring
that my room's always been.

Well, why not? After all,
life's long contest, for us,
has turned strained, serious.
Close and closer the call.

On Olympus Art's mother
keeps her pet, place and show
hard to judge as a star,
but here, loving each other,
it's easy to know
who the real winners are.

POETS IN LATE WINTER
For Joe Summers and Albert Lebowitz, birdwatchers

I

The poets of Missouri stare at astonishing winter.
On the windshields of their disabled cars they can see
rain, snow, hail, sleet, fog
all at once. Only the river still runs with pity.
The white sandwich they live on is snow between slabs of ice.
For three weeks no one can walk. Perhaps
sold-out salt will float in, they can sit beside
their stricken friend, iced in without guides or maps;
throw enough friction under their skidding souls
to pick up the news thrown on their own front yard
(One man who fell and lay helpless outside his door
clutched his paper and bellowed to wake his lifeguard,
who hunted the house up and down for her husband's voice);
can carry hot food to the trembling next-door widow
(self-immured for ten days from the poisonous glass)
without a steel-point stave to poke down to snow
while wearing golf shoes to crack-step across the lawn;
can send a serious verse to the humorist
who smashed her thirty-year-old hip. For three days
no mailman comes. Never was mail more missed.
Books and small screen pall, poems that hail
Into the cold mind coldly rattle like ping-pong.
In St. Louis seventy mailmen are hurt in falls
the day they try again. It goes on too long.

After two weeks the poets of Missouri hear
that their wintering-over birds are going to die.
For too long the inches of ice on top of snow
on top of ice have kept them from seeds, though they fly,
searching everywhere, through the freezing storms.
Each dried-berry-hung bush is iced off from a bill.
There is no water, each pond and stream stays solid.
Such innocent song to suffer the earth's ill-will!

In city, village, farm, frantic, the poets
set out to save the lovely reds and blues
of cardinal and jay, the cocky mocker,
junco, chickadee, waxwing . . . pulling their golf shoes
on and off all day, they balance warm water
again and again, fill feeders, their mittens smeared
with peanut butter, fat, raisins, breadcrumbs.
From wind and sorrow their face-scarves and eyes are teared.
And the little ones come from the woods, at least some, bedraggled,
too starved and thirsty to scare when food is thrown,
sparrows and starlings too, crows, pigeons, everybody.
Old bird books wake and call out birds unknown.
In his bright beret even the huge red-bellied
woodpecker hunches down to the holes of the feeders.
"If we stick together," he says to the poets of Missouri,
"The earth will re-print for its most devoted readers."

II

The poets of Missouri, in color, are dreaming
a T.V. drama that troubles their sleep:
when they sailed to these shores of being and seeming
they were met by a giant in exquisite motley
who became their faithful servant. Whatever
they asked he brought or did, though he
was mute except for a high little hum
(as he went about his magical work)
which they took to be happiness. Bang of drum
and now he appears, arms at his side,
dressed like a robot in Reynolds Wrap.
He is looking at them. Used to the big wide
billboards of human grief and desire,
they're unable to understand such a look.
Next a zoom to his heart. If he should aspire
to a heart, they supposed it crisp, firm, green
like Granny apple. But what runny chaos
is this that erupts all over the screen?

Whatever it was is now worn, rancid,
its form weakened by lack of care,
lack of gratitude, praise. Amid
its weary, mushy straining to live
are runnels of need and pain. Their paper
feelings crumple as they cry, "Forgive . . ."
How *could* they have guessed that the generous monster
loved them? The camera shifts and he turns
transparent. Heart fills his throat like fur.
"Our word, our world," they cry, "we've been wrong!"
He tries to hum again, but chokes up
and ends that tiny, unearthly song.

POETS' PAINT POTS

(On rereading Richard Wilbur's
"Two Voices in a Meadow" and
"Love Calls Us to the Things of This World")

"My poems are not Dick Wilbur!"
once snarled-up edicts of mine.
Time's tongue licked off dead fur
from their pelt to clear that line.

To the sill where such poems tower
no writer of them may aspire.
His own cripplings, power,
greed, coldness, fire,

almsgiving, grovels, pride,
footclay and ankle-wing
must lie like paint pots inside,
familiar, open for using.

He's locked from the highest address
so that bodiless words may relate
to the Denizen of that dorm,
to His spirit's perfect lightness,
and His perfect carnal weight,
alive in transparent form.

MINIMALIST SONNET TRANSLATIONS OF, OR COMMENTS ON, POEMS BY AUDEN, ELIOT, YEATS, FROST, HOPKINS, ARNOLD

COMMENT ON A LINE FROM AUDEN'S
"In Memory of William Butler Yeats"
For poetry makes nothing happen.

Tragic
indeed
should such magic
succeed!

Who made All,
word-hero,
must fall
to cause zero,

mind's breath
disproving,
bring by soundless
unloving
the death
of what's moving?

T. S. ELIOT's "The Love Song of J. Alfred Prufrock" (TRANSLATION)

While appalled
mirror
squeaks bald
terror

alone
unhat
her salon
chit-chat,

say "*Me,*"
"*I'll . . .*"
to sightsee
her smile?

Hardly
worthwhile . . .

W. B. YEATS' "The Circus Animals Desertion" (TRANSLATION)

Linking
starts
in stinking
hearts.

Dung
clings,
but rung
sings.

Then
rust.
Again
one must

think
stink.

YEATS' "A Prayer for My Daughter" (TRANSLATION)

Storm
violates.
Form
generates

deep
courtesy,
not cheap
beauty.

In bedroom
page,
her bridegroom,
image,

baring us
his toy,
outrageous
joy,

cauls
torn
so all's
fineborn,

let her be
poetry.

ROBERT FROST's "Mending Wall" (COMMENT)

In politics, arts
no issue's dramatic
nor will "play" till its heart's
simplified to fanatic.

All or None, Night and Day
call all else faddle-fiddle:
nothing moving is gray,
no ground has a middle.

Mute, helpless fact
may convince ages hence
life's most balanced act
is to stand on the fence.

For love is not peeing.
Mind's moves are not tides,
and each sentient being
bears the pain that resides
in feeling and seeing
at once, both sides.

HOPKINS' "Pied Beauty"   (TRANSLATION)

> What is clear in beauty
> years re-arrange,
> but its mystery
> keeps safe from change.
>
> Time can't critique
> paint brush dribbles
> nor freshness leak
> from a child's scribbles.
>
> Improvisations
> remake art's dater.
> In strange creations
> we glimpse the Creator:
>
> a free-form Thing,
> the first Happening.

MATTHEW ARNOLD's "Dover Beach"   (TRANSLATION)

> Sweetness
> seems.
> Mess
> screams.
>
> Be
> clone.
> We
> are alone
>
> in unfaith
> armed,
> wrath
> uncharmed,
>
> an ungirled
> world.

RASCASSE

In off-season chill, berthed yachts are spiking stems
into the plum-colored evening of the Harbor
outside the door. We attend our first authentic
bouillabaisse in Nice. On each table, *azur*
as the morning sea, a delicate white bouquet.
"What is that flower?" I ask the bowing blacktie,
his answer so startling I hear the English "I".
"*Pardon? . . . oh, ail. Vraiment? C'est charmant ici!*"
But we have not come for charm and blossom, but homeliness,
the deep, loamy musk of birth and decay
that hides from the eyes, the head of the garlic, the seed.

On the table rolled to ours a flat pan holds
the posed trio under a fiery arbor
of crabs, tails to a blue-black coil of conger.
On either side, like bridesmaids, the symmetry,
grace, sea-molded curves of mullet and loup;
in the center, the bride ("a first-class bouillabaisse
owes its quality to the *rascasse*, which is
essential"), *rascasse* the hog-fish, known to folk
and fishermen as the ugliest fish in the world.
Round, lovely eyes of her finny attendants
are blind to the rope of grotesque neck
that lifts a snouted face to her clan of lovers.

The surgeon-waiter bones with a click, click, click.
Over the flesh, divided and dealt, is poured
the broth of all, most prized for that one essence.

II
The eyes have led us astray through dreaming years,
cherishing consonance, curve, the colorful,
proportion, radiance, balance, harmony,
shapeliness that ages etched on our lenses.
We wed and bed the by-product, but spurn the essence.

Rascasse

We see the skin of the earth and it is beautiful,
but what formless fury fills earth's bowels and fuels us?
From Tennyson's "fire in the belly" sprang up poems.
Do the eyes want to look in the gut and know its essence?
From what came comfort of home, came fountain and spire?
From the mess of feeling, Yeats' "foul rag-and-boneshop."
What fertilizes but muck? What began us but slime?
We nod to the *belle-laide* with her troublesome half-truth,
but what gives comfort, what creates, but ugliness?

III
Suppose the light of the eyes went out and we walk
at a strange, cold moon's insistence into a place
bleached of curve, custom and color, down ways
of misty shapelessness. We walk for days
(or nights). The world, if it is a world, is empty.
No shadow befriends us, our soles press spongy silence.
Finally on some street (or field or shore)
we come to an ugly house and enter. There
we feel, and smell the stench of, some boggy burning.
We kneel at the edge of it and hold out our hands.
Then slowly a center inside us begins to glow
through loops, knots, clumps, from head to toe,
dusky alleys, wires, bags, stems,
and rosy comfort flowers through every pore
into inconceivable gardens. Light flares on our lessons.
We have knelt at the unpraised heart of being, of essence.

IV
The rich broth of life, whose bubble eyes
hold both the unseen and the seen, will defend it—
essence—ugliness (eh, *rascasse*?), comfort.
May all the color and beauty of the world attend it!

Quotation from *French Riviera, cote d'azur*, Michelin Tourist Guide

I I I

I'm not the least bit afraid of dying; I just don't want to be there when it happens. WOODY ALLEN

CLOSURES

Line fourteen
closes
to serene
supposes.
A sparkling
soda
toasts the darkling
coda.

Life's canvas
only
would revoke

the lustrous,
lonely,
last stroke.

"WE ARE IN YOUR AREA"

At every hour of morning to night my telephone
brings me the news that they are in our area
(or will be in our area by the next afternoon),
Veterans of every war, in every condition
("Judith, you've *got* to get off that phone a half hour,"
a friend told her teenage daughter. "I'm expecting a call
from Disabled American Veterans!") vying to pick up
kindly old clothes that have learned our old bodies,
old dear castiron skillets, the old chairs
we sit on, re- and re-covered since the fifties,
all Lighthouses for the Blind, all Handicapped Workers
who truck in more, still more, Everlasting Light Bulbs,
brooms and mops for our bulging shelves and closets,
Spreaders of Cement Patios who would disembarrass
our yard of its big warm brick one, Tuckpointers, Roofers,
Venders of the Latest Storm Window, Landscapers, Sweeps,
Construction and Remodelling groups in their urgent dozens
who would rip away our downstairs sideporch library
(where books of our friends nap in grownup silence
till we wake them up for a lively romp with our minds)
and nail on a family room for our long-lost children,
Cleaners of Carpets with Three-room, Ten-room Specials,
who disdain my expertise at pushing battered
sudsers and steamers rented from supermarkets,
Basement Waterproofers for our high, dry basement,
Driveway Glazers and Blacktoppers, Plasterers,
College Student Painting Services, pleading
to repaint the paint just spread by other such Students,
Tree Removers who would rid the birds and squirrels
of fruit and bloom I carefully planted and nurtured,
Lawn Care Specialists, scornful of amateur tending,
who poison, spray, feed and aerate on schedule.
While my husband cleans the gutters of the next-door widow
I am on the phone being wooed by yearning guttermen.

There is such a jam in our area of ghostly vans,
pickups and flatbeds there's nowhere to park our car,
such milling crowds of phantom workmen in frontyards
and backyards one hardly dares to go out the door
and enjoy the garden or feed the birds, such parades
of strange, invisible machines being brought to the houses
one can scarcely walk the dog, one fears for the mailman.
Neighbors' houses are shielded away from a visit
by unseen flying buttresses of ladders.
And, in such a silent bedlam of roaring, smashing,
hacking, pounding, jackhammering, sawing, hissing,
in our area one can hardly hear one'sself think.

II
But why aren't they in our area, why won't they come
when the furnace thermostat dies on the coldest weekend
of the whole winter, when a pipe rusts through and water
is pouring out of the ceiling, when treeroots squeeze
through the sewer pipe and grow into tangled clogs,
when all the lights in the neighborhood go out?
Without even a casual "See ya. ." they have slipped away
to another area where they are all booked up.
And why have they left our area, those tender young boys
with the proud, serious faces of first-time earners,
who will mow the lawn, wash cars, try to do anything?
They have moved far away to full-blown adolescence,
to driving and dates, they will not come back any more.
And why have they left, the long-time friends and neighbors
who moved many miles to country retirement homes
or to condos in far mushroom-bulging developments
which are hard to locate even with good directions?

And why, why, taking so much of ours with them,
have they left, those who always supplied us so freely
with our heat and light, those who drove clear off the maps
and left no directions? Soon we must set off to find
their precious, populous place, to be in their area.

ENDINGS

For Howard Nemerov

I

Sometimes when I read a book (verse or memoir,
novel, tales, travel, fat or slim)
a collapsed balloon seeps silently under the door,
sucks me in, inflates, and is once more
the world itself, or the world in my favorite guise—
a sly, reckless, outrageous poet who rhymes
its fiddleheads with its frost ferns, its starspace
with pasture, buttes with gullies, Cloud Ears with cliff-face.
In an air filled with this unearthly Muzak
of earth, a child, eyes wide, is lifted and held
for a first sight by arms of the artistry
that found the view and breathes "Look!" The child is me.
Innocent of endings as anyone at an
Introduction, the rapt mind gazes, sees,
clasped, in love's murmur, in the world's strange song.
But the right hand's wiser senses, all along,
ripping through timelessness, have begun to measure.
Between a thumb and fingers the ground grows thinner,
begins to glow with an efflorescence like pain.
See slowly! I beg my eyes, but again and again
the fingers feel how fast the time is coming
when arms will drop, the child fall through and be gone.
Even more terribly, footnotes, index or postscript
can fool the alarm so the trap is abruptly tripped.
"I cannot bear it," I think, but read on in a rage
for the rest of whatever it is, for the child, for the "Look!"
until the hand on which my heart is depending
holds only the blank page that follows an ending.

II

Setting the V.C.R. when we go to bed
to record a night owl movie, some charmer we missed,
we always allow, for unprogrammed unforeseen,
an extra half hour. (Night gods of the small screen
are ruthless with watchers trapped in their piety.)
We watch next evening, and having slowly found
the start of the film, meet the minors and leads,
enter their time and place, their wills and needs,
hear in our chests the click of empathy's padlock,
watch the forces gather, unyielding world
against the unyielding heart, one longing's minefield
laid for another longing, which may yield.
Tears will salt the left-over salad I seize
during ads, or laughter slow my hurry to pee.
But as clot melts toward clearness a black fate
may fall on the screen; the movie started too late.
Torn from the backward-shining of an end
that lights up the meaning of the whole work,
disabled in mind and feeling, I flail and shout,
"I can't bear it! I *have* to see how it comes out!"
For what is story if not relief from the pain
of the inconclusive, from dread of the meaningless?
Minds in their silent blast-offs search through space
—how often I've followed yours!—for a resting-place.
And I'll follow, past each universe in its spangled
ballgown who waits for the slow-dance of life to start,
past vacancies of darkness whose vainglory
is endless as death's, to find the end of the story.

EXTRA TIME

Today the morning paper's nearly buried
under a whole dumped bagful of an "Extra"—
crisp, tan scrolls of the *Sycamore Times*,
whose headline is, as always, TIME TO GROW!
The grass, the weeds, the petunias, who believe
everything they read in the paper have shot up

an inch or more since yesterday. What goes up
must come down, I might have told them, but I buried
the words behind a smile even I could believe.
These warm, late days, a mysterious extra
is in the air, and should the old ground grow
too cold too soon the last laugh may not be Time's.

Reading the Want Ads first, how many times
have I made my way backward and ended up
with good news? Rarely. A sensible heart would grow
tired of celebrating some item buried
once in a while in the middle, of finding the extra-
ordinary so easy to believe

that it pastes on the dummy front page of what I believe
those trivial clippings that contradict the times.
A heart so unwearied, with very little extra
effort, could, it seems to me, dig up
the tons of newsprint that *it* has always buried,
dampen, compress, carve them until they grow

cold and hard as iceblocks. One could grow
inside such an igloo, grow cool enough to believe
oneself in the long twilight, forget the buried
sun, grow slow and padded with the blubber that sometimes,
from under its calm white, the deep yields up,
live without color, an earlier world's lost extra.

On a minimalist page every image is extra.
In an Arctic age only the mind can grow
sharp enough to skin and bone and slice up
to dry the meager meat that one must believe.
In darkness no one can find and follow Time's
footsteps to where the imagination is buried.

Or might one grow up enough to believe what's there
in black and white, yet feel Time's heavy steps
as extra, the heart's path to a buried light?

FROM THE MANTEL

Out of Mexico
an owl gazes past art,
past a livingroom's mart,
past a world at window,

to the source of snow,
hurting the heart
as its beauties impart
what is cruelly so:

all one must know
with such wide eyes,

the grace one can show
at each dark surprise,

the helpless sorrow
of being wise.

FOR MAY SWENSON

The world beside this one, imagination's egg,
rolls close to cuddle in our orbiting
(its shell impermeable to body or eye)
and inhales, like the feathered warmth of a spread wing
the forms that come forth fresh from their fiery making.

Tibetan Buddhists chant the names of things
"moonflower . . shell . . turquoise . . mountain . . sea"
to make "a perfect symbolic world . . a world
re-imagined . . recreated," * one that might be.
Out of a sprawling Mormon family,

riding a stick horse, the child, pug-nosed,
tow-haired, came to the place her life lay
deep in a slough of words and dredged there. Up
came the unheated shelter, the real name "May,"
the pride and peace of poems, their elegant play,

one warm and human love ("She was a true
hermit," Zan said) and all the beautiful furred,
winged, three-toed, four-toed, finned beings
that jewel the world. A belated grant assured
a year of "warmth and animals," the Great Bird.

Back home, she spent the morning on a poem,
playing with the young cat, scratching its cheek
to make it purr. Did she, above the purring,
hear the long-remembered *tick, tick, tick,*
the always miraculous signal of a beak?

Who knows? When a roughly star-shaped beam of light
from a chipped-out aperture blinded the wit
on the page, she put the cat and notebook down,
moved quietly to that shining, intimate
open place in the shell and entered it.

* "Imagining the Ocean," Jennifer Atkinson, *Threepenny Review*

AT THE MALL

The Young plot
each glance
but know chance
will allot

a moonshot
of romance,
a slowdance
of pot,

not hearing
life's handcuffs
unlock

till wearing
their earmuffs
of Rock.

SONDRA

Your high, soft voice, whenever you startled out
some hiding, hulking absurdity, became
still higher when you laughed, and higher still,
more bells than voice, until the highest chime
was shaken. The holocaust of your disease
chose early to take your voice and left till last
your dark eyes and the notes you wrote still glowing
with humor, with radiant memories of the past.
Racing the stomach tube with packed purées
of the most exotic tastiness I could find
(which your husband sieved and sieved against your choking)
I read that one reminded you of a kind
of white Gazpacho you had loved in Spain.
You asked for "the golden-spiced golden potato
soup" for breakfast. Your doctor's "star patient"
shooting to death, too soon you couldn't swallow.

Sondra, I remember you on the outskirts
of faculty parties, mind sheathed, immersed
in the three children at home, leaving early
to soothe their homework, problems, pains, but first,
dark eyes watching, lips in a secret smile.
"Sondra sees *everything*," I said in half-fun.
("My hair's turned gray! Now what?" "I guess one either dyes
or one doesn't." Your pride rose up, "But *I* am not '*one*'!")
True. Beyond their childhood a great cook,
beyond their schooling pianist once again;
your Bechstein ate up most of the diningroom;
your accompaniments shone forth onstage. Then
part-time professor, whose best student was always
not "my best student," but "my most brilliant" one,
as if you could see each facet already cut
on the young gemstone. Then a writer. Attention
followed your pen's point to Ford Madox Ford,
bright cooking with three ingredients, a new
approach to freshman writing.

Sondra

                                  Your soft, high voice
in patterns of party chatter came threading through
with quips and anecdotes: "When I first went
with Dick I thought I was rebelling, I thought
he was Chinese. When I learned he was the Jew
my parents prayed for I was already caught.
I loved him." "When I was young and something bad
happened to me on the city streets, instead
of going to my parents I'd write a letter
to the *Times*." Both of us left unsaid
what never needed saying, found ourselves
attracted to the same men, agreed
on lights and darks in our women friends. The disease
outwitted armies of science in its need
for prisoners, but not the armies of love
led by your doctor and your family.
"How can I get out of this box?" you wrote,
and so, with their tender skills, they set you free.

What have you left for us? Young scholar, young artist,
young lover of people. A husband whose brimming eyes
drown our hearts. Fine books. And where are you?
Hidden in what remains to us of sunrise.
Now, when the world's slippery, solemn arrangements
slide to a comic pratfall and quickly after
right themselves so nothing is badly hurt,
dear ghost, I hear the ghostly bells of your laughter.

INSIDERS

Within
the stout
a thin
wants out,

but a child
in the gray's
reconciled,
wants to stay,

so happy
to bicker
and win,

to be
in that thicker
skin.

CAPS

In the village café
all the men wear their caps
and with ritual backslaps
share out their day.

The nursinghome nurses
each time all were fed,
ignoring its curses,
tore its cap from one head

that tried to make normal
a curious hell,
in the packed dining-dome

to be mannerly, formal,
knowing perfectly well
it was not at home.

EMERGENCY ROOM

(Turnpike, Anywhere, U.S.A.)

The patient coffee machine urinates
endless specimens into little white cups
for testers who find
something indeed is terribly wrong,
but never remember to send their reports to doctors
who could, perhaps, treat the condition.

The big soft drinker in the corner
is obsessed with her female operation.
She keeps saying to herself and anyone who will listen,
"They took everything out. I just feel so *empty*."
The experienced leave her alone, but the innocent
come up to her, offer warm conversational coin,
but expect something in return,
some womanly soothing for their *own* needs.
She only repeats her one statement, ". . . . so *empty*,"
until they feel like kicking her.
Some of them do.

The normally hot-blooded soup is stiff from chill,
the iceberg lettuce salad is limp from fever.
Side by side in their bins,
passing the time by chatting away,
they think they may suffer from the same disorder.
"I don't feel at all like myself." "You do look awful."
"They let us sit here all day without any attention."
"Maybe an icepack would help you."
"You've got to keep yourself good and warm."
"It's obviously something going around."
"I hear it's a regular epidemic."

Emergency Room

Left on a table to die, a sandwich
can hardly believe this has happened to him.
Having heard it said so often about
his friends and neighbors, he still never expected
his own epitaph to be:
"They opened him up, took one look,
and just closed him up again."

In an adjoining section sufferers can see
disjointed bits of medical training taking place.
A long, nearly unmoving queue of them
suggests that primarily women, these days,
wish to be surgeons.
Each comes out, after what must have been
a long, laborious scrub,
looking annoyed, holding her dripping hands
well away from body and shoulderbag,
shaking them violently to dry in the air,
since the snappers-on of the rubber gloves
must be practising someplace else.

The male trainees shoot expeditiously in and out
of another door behind which must be required
only the briefest demonstration
of some minor but useful skill—
perhaps of assuming the look of dignified relief
and self-satisfaction,
the look that is still on the face of each when he exits,
that, when he's fully qualified, announces
to waiting relatives from far down the hall
"Yes, a-a-ah yes,
everything came out well."

LATE WISHES

Scientific, I only
wished I'd wed an M.D.,
who could forecast the lonely
departure of Me.

But of late, realistic,
I think I'd much rather
have married the mystic
who predicts the weather.

Though the whimsical sky
toss down grim absolutes

with the proper supply
of bikinis or boots

a whole canton and I
could go out in cahoots.

STRUGGLE TOWARD A NARRATIVE

One livingroom window suddenly darkens. Her eyes startle up from her notebook. A gray-black monster, wings spread and flapping, covers the window, or the lower half of it, pressing against the glass. She has been waiting for news of the death of a friend. But why has it come in this frightful way?

His last words to her, four or five days earlier, were "Let's stay in communication. I'll let you know how it comes out." But he was talking about something else, something he planned to do in his last functioning days before the recent doses of morphine took him into silence. Surely it was only her keyed-up, oversensitized mind that had linked his words with some lines of a poem on closures that she had written him in his illness: "Torn from the backward-shining of an end/ that lights up the meaning of the whole work,/ disabled in mind and feeling I flail and shout,/ "I can't bear it! I *have* to see how it comes out!" The doctor had said that his heart and lungs and digestion were still strong, that he might linger for some time. Was this unrecognizable horror at the window the only way he could reach her? She screams for her husband, who runs from his sandwich in the kitchen, "Come here quick, something terrible is happening!"

> *Unplug from their old, defective sockets eyes*
> *whose iridescent Rorschachs sluggishly rise*
> *like bubbles from a private swamp and break*
> *the stillness of appearances that would make*
> *its seeming into solid; touch disguise*
> *with humbler senses, much stranger to mistake.*

He walks to the window. He: "It's a crow. But why is it hanging on the window screen?" She: "No. Where's its head? There's only a body and wings. Crows aren't *that* big." He: "They are up this close, flapping their wings. It's the only bird that *could* be that big." She is able to join him at the window. She: "Oh, I see its head. It's twisting its neck backwards and looking down. Why doesn't it go away? That's not a crow, its breast is all furry and gray, like an animal rather than a bird." He: "It must be hurt and can't fly. Oh look, there are two crows in the air chasing it and squawking at it. They keep darting down at it. They must be attacking a hurt crow, chickens will do that—peck a hurt chicken to death." She: "Crows wouldn't attack another crow, they're social birds. It *must* be another kind of giant bird and it's invaded their territory. Look, its head and beak are not shaped quite like a crow's and it's the wrong color, at least on its front."

In the black surround of chaos whirlwinds of wish
roar in silence. Every satellite dish
of the Unconscious trembles with their need,
those yearning exiles from shape, from weight of deed,
from sight, from rot and rose of flesh, from anguish.
Forever the spirit wants to be embodied.

The bird twists its head up to look briefly at them, then looks back and down. She has seen the beak clearly. She: "Oh my God, it's a *baby*! A young crow. Those are its parents, they're hysterical about it. They're not attacking, they're trying to protect it. But why is it trying to get in the window?" She steps closer. She: "Oh honey, it's caught in the screen. See those little curved wire toenails hooked in the screen. It can't get off. Oh, do something quick. You've got to get hold of it somehow without hurting it and fold its wings and unhook its nails. Oh, the poor thing, it's holding that huge, heavy body up with its tiny little toenails. Go out and try to help it, quick!" He moves slowly and reluctantly toward the door. She: "Or maybe we need a towel to wrap it quiet while we unhook its nails so they won't break off . . ."

A wild invention, shoving into the gape
of unguarded childhood, Zeus's double rape,
as Rilke has it, to make himself again!
Out of abstract knowledge and power, warm semen
shot from a swan too young to claim his inscape,
but who "verily became swan" through the human hen.

She moves still closer to the window as he hesitates at the door, and now is able to see the ground three feet directly below the bird. In the vinca ground cover, eyes fixed intently on the enormous prey, is crouched the neighbor's calico cat, named "Cat." She yells: "*Quick,* Cat's under the bird, chase her away. *Quick!*" He knows what to do now, shoots out the door, shouting and clapping his hands, "*Get away*, Cat! *Shoo!*" running at the cat, who streaks toward home and disappears. The bird drops to the ground. In a few moments one of the parent crows lights on the ground and leads the limping young bird away. Although it obviously cannot fly adequately, it is almost as big as its parent. He comes back in, triumphant. They collapse side by side in their chairs. He: "*Well . . .*" She: "What a relief! But how helpless those great big birds were in protecting their child—a mockingbird would have had that cat out of there in a minute." He: "Or a little tiny redwing blackbird at the golf course. They hit our heads like a hammer when we're near their nests." She: "Well . . . we saved it . . ." He: "Yes . . . but do we really want more crows? You know what a pest they are, pecking holes in the garbage bags we have to leave out for the pickups, strewing garbage all over . ." She: "Yes . . no . . . no, we don't need more crows. But think how frantic the parents were. And do we want to see the killing of something helpless that we could have saved? He: "Yes . . Well, of course not." She: "But it took so long for us to know what was happening. I hope his poor toes and nails are not broken. Maybe something will get him when we don't see it. He: "Yeah . . well . . we certainly don't need more crows."

> At the dreary midnight of death the weary raven
> tells his story to the nearest haven,
> finding his way by rote to that open door:
> "Never again will I be, nor was ever before."
> No art is needed to keep a life that is graven
> on a tiny moment before the long Nevermore.

Waking early next morning, unable to go back to sleep, she is drinking tea when the phone rings. Her friend died at midnight in spite of the doctors' prediction.

> "Why is Eros always shown in the form
> of a babe?" he had once mused. "It came to me
> that He stands for the unborn child who wants to be born."

Adrift on the drug, sometimes he groans. They've sworn
it's not pain. Labor, contractions of flesh, as what
is ineffable swells till its alleyway is torn?

"Habit of being" leads an unsaid "goodnight"
toward words, toward morning's brilliant speech of light.

FALLEN ANGEL

For   *Ray*
       Sandy
       Sondra
       May
       Leanna
       Mary
       Tom H.
       (DEATH'S SIX-MONTH HARVEST)

Not from rebellion does the angel fall.
The muscles of its pinions are huge from the stress
of storms that beat against its blessedness,
its migrations to need, whose distances are deceitful.

Its body, blurred as a hummingbird's, is light,
as if it were made of light, so beautifully
does it drift in flight into the inward country
to rise and dip with the winging blindness or insight.

If we could not believe that it was there
above the stifling trees, below the stars
that are unmoved by our dreadful strain at bars
that block our shining in answer, wish would outwear.

The angel comes, over and over. But one day
before we know it, out of our sight or will,
its plumes are wilted in the air by an oilspill
that blots its flight-path and cannot be skimmed away.

The feathery Word blackens and shrivels, the body
is rigid and heavy, covered with an icy mail,
turned to such a burden the wing muscles flail,
and a cloud shifts, unmasking the enemy.

Then the angel begins to fall, for all its glory.
Its shimmering talents hang like tarnished coin.
Its wonder weights it. Like sinkers, letters join.
MELO - links to its dramatic story,

Its sentiment must carry - ALITY.
It drops faster, writhing less and less,
toward the trite, foreknown crash to nothingness,
scarring the sky with its sharp, mute agony.

But the kind re-Creator of the human sphere
has spread over vast reaches a pillowed place
to receive its plummet, cosset its crumpled grace.
Gazing through glass shaped like a monstrous tear

that will wash lies, darkness and rubbish from the form
of the falling angel, I saw once from far above
the Alps an image of that place of love.
Baked by a master, exquisite, chaste, warm,

to its utmost edges the ground had been undone
for a thousand-peaked meringue, the tender peaks
pulled from the fire so quickly their delicate streaks
of tan had barely dried on the soft white welcome.

Everywhere beneath it, the peaks it can see
are lifting, lifting themselves to break its fall,
and the angel smiles and sinks, safe for us all,
in a grave, sweet, sticky foam of memory.

A CERTAIN AGE

Say "May I?"
the child
is told by
her mild

exegete
is the way
to the sweet,
to the play.

But I'm
abused
since Time
refused

to say
I may.

THE POET RECONCILES HERSELF TO POLITICIANS
Politics is, as it were, the gizzard of society,
full of grit and gravel. THOREAU

The sharp and the coarse
grind our life into law,
dealing by force
with the heart's monstrous maw.

Wormy riches, pride's weed,
the hot mash of sex,
power's cold chickenfeed,
earned by bloody head-pecks—

Since fineness can't chasten
the internal roister
that greed gobbled raw,
let stony clods hasten,
or our great only oyster
may stick in our craw.

FALLS

There, where I lived a quarter century, there was nothing
to look up for (oh, a perfect apple turning ripe
on one of the backyard trees, or a sudden new
birdnest), nothing ever in the sky but weather,
nothing for weather to do there but make corn
forever "knee-high by the fourth of July."
Anger, resentment, self-pity, what were they
but weeds to be chopped out fast to make more room for the
crop, the only crop that rich land wanted.
Beauty in the soft backdrop of green hill-breasts
Grant Wood hung behind burned, bony faces?
If you saw that, then "You'd better get your head
on straight!" Only now can trained young eyes
who come from "away" utter in wonder, "He didn't
stylize a bit, he painted literally!"
Wildflowers were deadened into ragged dust-humps
at the edge of gravel roads whose stinging, blinding
clouds kept cars apart from one another.
Narrow, two-laned pavement let the corn
come marching in its stiff green to the very edge,
grudging the trail its ground. Our only travel:
a Sunday's forty gravel miles to dear Grandma's
village or Aunt's farm. Rarely, a Sunday
trip to Dad's folks, fifty miles to the Town
(those pious strangers who stiffly smiled at "little
Monna Jane," who never felt like me).
Rolling on paving between flat fields of green,
prized stalks, once or twice a frizzy yellow-
green of willows scribbled a wandering creek.
Sometimes there were miles of the stomach-heaving
stench of fields just fertilized with shit,
or cry of "Peeuuu! Skunk! Skunk got hit!"
and sometimes rising and falling above the cornrows
(like a waterfall of pure sound?) "Oh, Meadowlark!"
But what was a waterfall? It seemed to me
that more than "ocean" or "mountain" I wanted to see
the wonder-welling of a waterfall.

74

How could I ever have guessed my father's dream,
who never was vouchsafed his simplest thought?
A gangling high school junior, I was told
he'd bought a newfangled "trailer house" which, hitched
to our car would waft us to the Western Sea.

Near dark the three of us stood with a crowd, looking up
from a hill off to the side of Yosemite's
great cliff where, after already blurred marvels
undreamed-of, my father's dream had brought us to be.
The top of the cliff was darker than the sky,
which slowly darkened to meet it till everywhere
was darkness of sky, the mind went dark, one stood
completely alone, breath held. It began: The Firefall.
Out of some secret opening in the sky
the first blazing streaks began to pour
toward earth, the rent in darkness widened and widened
to let fall a dazzling creek, then more and more
cascaded down the dark until a full
river of radiance from abstemious heaven
made its slow unbroken, quivering reach
for whatever bed on unknown ground would be given.
Who could have guessed from what some careless hand
had broadcast—those few tiniest, dimmest sparks
in the dark soil of the sky—that the sky was hiding
more brilliance than it could hint at, a hidden lark
whispered perhaps of things called symphonies.
How long was the Firefall? Time had kept its sands
from falling. What was the fire? Although it fell
from the soul's home and braided into its strands
of hue and heat that cool, unearthly white,
its glory poured from earth's burning body, red,
yellow, blue, orange, twining, twisting
to light, to stainless light. But no riverbed
lay below to lead it over the earth
and make its wonder a lasting link with heaven.

Falls

So close to heaven was the lip of the Fall, so light
the limbs that spun, locked, spun, even
so long and lovely was the fall toward solid ground
that, its parts one by one winking out in air
imperceptibly, the Firefall died from the very
breath of earth that begot its celestial flare.
On the ground below us no smouldering heaps glowed up.
Park lights went on. We walked home from the hill.
I walked toward what I had never before imagined,
hearing my own heart's life, its fill and refill.

"College? What's the good of your going to college?
No, I haven't got that kind of money!"
Months of tears. "All right, you get yourself
a scholarship to the State Teachers College,
come home on weekends—otherwise, no college."
Books! No classes in psychology
so I could learn what normal people were like,
but Books! Soon I got free run of the stacks,
the nice old ladies trying to teach classes
liked me and let me read. The god who wrote
poems and showed them to me gave me lists
of poets and novelists, called me a writer,
let me love-worship-adore him (first love
that lasted his life long), gave me one burning
kiss that changed the color of the sky,
left for a better job and wrote me heart-felt letters.
Weekends at home I read. "You've got to stop
that reading, it's going to make you lose your mind.
You're too big-headed already!" Refrain from **Dad.**
Two lasting hilarities: out of my lists
of authors I chose *Finnegan's Wake* as a first
dip into Joyce. Grand-style bewilderment!
For first James I plucked *The Golden Bowl*
from the shelf, read with total pleased absorption,
reached the end and only then woke up

to ask myself, "What in the world did I read?
What happened?" A new and lasting humility!
Poems I read by thousands rolled in my mind
like rocks, polished against each other, crumbling
to chips and dust only in late old age.
In summer before my sophomore year began
my father hitched the trailer up for the East.
Parked in the back yard of a relative
in calm New Jersey, we saw the World's Fair,
and, more to my poem's point, Niagara Falls.
Smirks from the relatives. "You know that's where
the honeymooners go? Well, guess it won't
be long before *you* go without your folks.
College girl, eh? Well, you'll get over that."

We walked toward a roar that reached beyond the senses.
No waterfall, it seemed, but earth's bringing together
of all its waters to make for that monstrous, open
mouth (one lip one country, one another),
out of a thousand long white quivering tongues
one tongue that brought from the depths of throat appalling,
thunderous boasts of its own fertility.
Unceasing, day and night, with its giant calling
shaking the shoulder we stood on with its passion,
the earth poured law to our puny selves, which shrank
to the size of a seed as in the roar of its will
it sucked from us our watery dross and drank.
"This is no waterfall for the newly-wed,"
I knew within myself. "First the Firefall,
then, years later, here." We drove to see
the American lip from Canada's side, but the whole
was beyond the grasp of my lens and I snapped instead
a family of swans, a simpler sight,
father, mother, puffball babies, strolling.
At home I printed underneath in white
on the black album page, *Swans En Famille*,

proud of my first-year French. Prescient, perhaps,
but, with no course in Earth, I had read the roar.
"*Life!*" Life and more life I want! Not *one* crop
but *thousands* in their unimaginable
abundance, shape, size, color, kind—*all*
the undreamed-of, the yet to come, my body will bear.
I tell my own truth in my waterfall."
Gradually we drove toward silence. Years
went by and a time came when I heard the roar
and eagerly bent my head to the waters' will
that filled my fleshy chambers to their core.
Wild for the blind, helpless confinement to send me
over the lip in a will-less fall, thrown
from my safe, observant stand, tossed, rammed,
broken, drowned perhaps—but love alone,
however strong and skilled, could build no barrel.
My field unamplified as the voice of one bird's
in the corn, I fall, rise, praise, fall,
sowing and tilling my single crop— Words. Words.

May one who comes upon a final book
and hunts in husks for kernel hints of me
find Niagara's roar still sacred to dim ears,
Firefall still blazing bright in memory.

See Note 2 on page 83

THE DELIVERY

I'm five. The petals of my timeless play
can unfurl while Mother hoes out other gardens.
The next-door child and I, alone with my toys,
confine to the diningroom our discreet noise.
From the doorway: "*Betty, come here!*" The uprooted flower
falls dead with no warning. What had my friend done,
rolled a dimestore car over the table top,
stood on a chair to wave the little dustmop?
I will never know. She is tethered to Mother's hand
and Mother's voice begins the long scolding.
I start a soldier's march around and around
the table, stomping each foot to stomp out her sound.
Faster around I stomp until it is over,
Betty is gone and Mother takes hold of me.
"What's the *matter* with you? Why is your face so red?
Why, you're *crying*, your whole face is dripping wet!
Well, if that isn't silly, I'd like to know what is!
I wasn't scolding *you*, I was scolding *Betty*."
She laughs. "Go wash your face." The room blears.
My hand wipes and finds all the unfelt tears.

Soon it is supper time. In the kitchen they feed
and talk, while I, invisible as I was
in high-chair days, silently sit on Sears,
wearing the weight of my big and bigger ears.
"Well, you'll never guess what your crazy kid did today—
if that wasn't the limit!" The story swells
into ache in my stomach, then Dad's laughter and hers
slice and tear like knives and forks and a worse
hurt is opening in my middle; in familiar
smells and muddle of voices, mashed potatoes,
dimming light, hamburger, thick creamed corn,
the milk-white chill, a self is being born.

And is swept away through seething clots of minnow
in the nearly hidden creek that weeps through the meadow,
smeared with mud from its suckling roots of willow,
to tributary, to river, deep and slow,
whose sob-like surges quietly lift her and carry
her unjudged freight clear to the mourning sea.
And there they are, all of the heavy others
(even Mother and Father), the floundering, floating or sinking
human herd, whose armstrokes, frail, awry,
frantic, hold up their heads to inhale the sky,
which gilds the tongues of water or soothes them to stillness
with white silk covers strewn with onyx and pearl.
She is with them, inept dog-paddler that she is.
The heavens whirl and drift their weightless riches
through streaky splendors of joy, or bare unending
lodes of blazing or ice-blue clarity.
With them all, all, she is scraped by crusted rock,
wrenched by tides untrue to heart or to clock,
fighting the undertow to shapelessness
in smothering deeps, to what is insufferable.
If those she can reach go under she cannot save them—
how could she save them? Omnipotent dark has seized them.
She can only sink with each one as far as light
can enter, meet drowning eyes and flesh still spangled
with tiny gems from above (a sign of the rare
her watered eyes never need), pointing to where,
up, in the passionate strain, lives everything fair
before she flails back to the loved, the illumined, air.

NOTES

1.   The short poems in this book are minimalist sonnets along with a few I have baptized (oxymoronically, perhaps), extended minimalist sonnets.

Of all the forms, the sonnet seems most available to poets for deconstruction. Meter, rhyme scheme, division into octave and sestet, turn in thought, all have at one time or another been dispensed with by writers, and any poem of fourteen lines has been called a sonnet. In my own play with the form, I have shortened the conventional iambic pentameter line in varying degrees, some of the sonnets being held to a one-accent line; but I have kept all other conventions of the Shakespearean, Petrarchan or Spenserian. The one convention that has remained constant through the years, the fourteen line length, I have, however, occasionally broken by adding an extra four lines. I have found the shortened line and the additional quatrain (the extended minimalist sonnet) make for a form that is a pleasure to work with and—I hope—to read.

2.   Because younger readers of "Falls" have been puzzled by what the firefall was, supposing it to have been the Northern Lights or some other natural phenomenon, a note may be useful. It was (in 1937, when I saw it, and as late as the 1950's, when a color photograph was taken) a nightly entertainment for tourists at Yosemite National Park, in which burning embers from what must have been an enormous bonfire were skillfully and continuously pushed over the top of a high cliff, creating in the dark a "waterfall" of fire. Anyone wishing to read a bit more about the Yosemite firefall is referred to *The Tourist at Yosemite, 1855–1985*, S. E. Demars, University of Utah Press, 1991.